Contents

Introduction 2
Chapter 1: Today Isn't Everything, Really 4
Chapter 2: Set The Goal Now, For Tomorrow's Benefit 7
Chapter 3: Growing And Staying Green 11
Chapter 4: Understanding Your Market 16
Chapter 5: Trend Versus Trend Setter 20
Chapter 6: Principal: History 24
Chapter 7: Investing In Knowledge 28
Chapter 8: Growth Success Without Potential Waste 33
Chapter 9: Managing Money Principles 37
Chapter 10: Marketing For True Success 44
Chapter 11: Principles To Remember And Use 50

Introduction

What does being an entrepreneur represent to you?

Anyone interested in achieving genuine success in their lives can accomplish this with the appropriate tools, sufficient ambition, and the knowledge to bring it all to fruition. However, an entrepreneur, regardless of the business they are involved in, must strategize and seek success through much more than just these elements.

As an entrepreneur, you are not merely pursuing immediate gains. While you certainly desire your business to thrive and perform well in its initial year, its early stage, it is equally important, if not more so, that your long-term objectives align with your current needs.

In the long run, the entrepreneur's environment is considerably different and uniquely distinct. To attain genuine success, one must consider both today and tomorrow—double the focus.

How and what steps will you take to ensure that your business, which you have diligently strived to establish, will endure in the long run? Although this task may not be simple, it is achievable with the right approach.

In this e-book, you will discover some of the most crucial principles for safeguarding your business not only for the present but also for the future.

As a new or aspiring entrepreneur, you may not have contemplated what lies ahead because only the present mattered. However, now is an ideal moment to reflect and determine the best strategy for managing your business over the long haul.

If you want a business that facilitates success and financial gain in the future, it is vital that you dedicate some time now to plan for it to materialize.

The positive aspect is that you do not need to attend school or be exceptionally intelligent to understand this. Indeed, we offer a substantial amount of information and resources that you require right here, without the necessity of seeking alternative sources.

Of course, we also hope you feel motivated to take the next step and uncover the genuine advantages of your business by implementing these strategies as a priority. When you take these actions, true success and financial stability will be what matters most.

Chapter 1: Today Isn't Everything, Really

As an entrepreneur, your responsibilities are highly complex. You are required to be the creative one. You need to take charge. You must keep your business vision at the forefront of all your actions for that endeavor. Nonetheless, today is not everything.

As a business owner, you must recognize that the long-term goals and operations of your business can only be achieved if you plan for it now, instead of merely focusing on the present.

You may have heard people advise you that you should; "Live in the day!" As an entrepreneur, this is impractical and should not shape your business strategy.

But, why is this the case?

Frequently, we tend to think that all we need to do is devise a plan and adhere to it. Somehow, things will fall into place. They have to. That's all that is achievable.

However, from a business standpoint, there is significantly more to consider.

For example, there might be employees who depend on the income generated by your business for their daily living costs.

You must contemplate the overall benefits of maintaining your business. What about your resources? Will they endure this process? What is your cash flow status? What might occur if a problem arises?

All of these issues are just the start of the hurdles that could threaten a business in the long run. The essential point is that you must think about how your business will appear today and in ten, twenty years, and beyond.

Think About This

Before we move forward, it is crucial that you understand two concepts relevant to your business operations. When making a decision in your business, first consider the following questions.

1. When I make this decision, what are the short-term and immediate ramifications of doing so? How does this affect my business today?

2. When I make this decision, what are the long-term implications of making this choice? How will this decision impact my business in the months and years ahead?

By taking the time to carefully assess the decisions in front of you, you exert control over your future.

If you allow circumstances to dictate the result, you could find yourself without a business in six months. Therefore, as you go through this e-book, reflect on what actions you can take immediately that will improve your overall business both now and in the future.

Certainly, it is important to remember that there is never a certain way to foresee what the future holds. There is no method to determine whether you are genuinely making the right decision or not. Nevertheless, what you need to do in this situation is ensure that you provide tomorrow with the best possible chance that you can.

Do not allow it to merely happen; make today meaningful for tomorrow and for the day after tomorrow as well.

Chapter 2: Set The Goal Now, For Tomorrow's Benefit

Regardless of the area of your life being discussed, setting goals is a vital element in all areas. As you will observe, every choice you make as an entrepreneur will impact your overarching objective of achieving success in your business. However, it extends beyond just that.

You ought to establish goals since they can assist you in making the appropriate choices during the journey toward the success that lies ahead. By dedicating the necessary time and effort to set goals now, you better equip yourself for every decision needed to attain the desired outcome.

In simpler terms, by establishing some broad goals today, you can help ensure that your business will thrive and flourish throughout its future. Goals set now are significant.

Although we all share the common aim of achieving future success, we must still define goals to guide us to that destination. It does not occur instantaneously!

How To Set Goals Successfully

When it comes to goal-setting, not many of us excel at it. There are numerous chances for errors to arise, but the main issue lies in the manner in which we establish them and what actions we take after setting them.

To start, it is important to identify what your goals are. Take a few moments right now to determine this. Simply sit with a blank sheet of paper (yes, a computer is acceptable too!) and eliminate all distractions for ten minutes.

Note down any and everything that pops into your head regarding your goals.

What are your goals?
Where do you aspire to be in a year?
Who do you wish to have alongside you?
Where do you envision your business in five years? 20?
What sales figure would satisfy you this year?
What profit do you need to achieve a new level of satisfaction each year?

All these queries may spark your thoughts. Identify where you foresee your business being in the coming years. Start with a long-term perspective. Then, apply these suggestions.

Writing down your goals becomes straightforward with a few fundamental steps.

1. Document your most distant goal. This represents the destination you aim to reach in several years or the state you need to achieve to attain the level of success you envision.

2. Establish a timeframe for achieving that. You might decide that

you wish to earn your first million within two years. Alternatively, it could take significantly longer to achieve that. Setting a timeframe for your goal aids in mentally preparing for how to reach it. If you leave it indefinite, your daily actions will not effectively support your long-term goals as they would in this scenario.

3. Set smaller goals to attain as steps towards the larger one. For instance, the aspiring entrepreneur might express a desire to have an office established and operational within a month. In six months, he aspires to be generating profit after covering expenses. Identify what your steps are to achieve your goal. Ensure to document them with corresponding timeframes as well.

4. Now, write them out by hand on paper in this specific way. "Within six months, I will have eliminated all the debt I owe and will be operating profitably. I will achieve this by increasing sales and avoiding any new expenditures during that period. " By doing this, you not only outline the goal and the timeframe for its completion, but also convey the approach you will take to reach it.

5. Take this written document and place it in multiple locations where you will notice it several times each day. Observing it will enable you to contemplate it. Contemplating it makes it a reality. Achieving success through goals is the sole pathway to attain it.

Now that you have identified your goals, it is crucial to ensure their realization.

You should aim to review those goals daily, at least once per day. When you think about it, visualize it, and feel it, you make it come to fruition.

In the following chapters, we will explore the long-term decisions you need to make as well as various actions you should undertake to facilitate them.

As you progress through each step, identify your goal for it. How will you incorporate it into your existing work routine, and how will you ensure its execution?

Chapter 3: Growing And Staying Green

When you are green, you are in a state of growth. Once you begin to turn red, you are nearing the end. Don't you desire to remain green indefinitely?

As an entrepreneur, one thing you should understand is that the world is always changing. For the most part, you will consistently encounter changes. As a business owner, if you are unable to adapt your business to these changes, you may find yourself experiencing more challenges than advantages.

Numerous companies have gone out of business solely because their products no longer align with consumer needs. It does not matter what kind of business you operate. The essential point is that if you are not green and growing, you will not survive in business for long.

Is your business green and growing?

The Long Term Goal

The long term goal of any business scenario is to ensure that they can fulfill the needs of the client or consumer. If they fail to do this, they cannot retain consumers and will ultimately fall out of favor. If they succeed, they will continuously reap rewards with increased profits and new clients to support their growth.

In this case, the long term objective you need to set is to remain green. You must maintain some aspect that will continually assist you in progressing with the developments occurring within your business.

If you are uncertain why this is crucial, consider the current situation.

Enter The Car Manufacturing Business

Nowadays, we hear a lot of discussions regarding energy costs, gas prices, and everything related. In fact, more people today are aware of the price of a barrel of crude oil than ever before. Why is this, and what impact does it have on the industry?

If you haven't dedicated any time to shopping for a car, you may not recognize that many manufacturers are struggling to remain operational. Their challenge is that their cars, trucks, or anything in between are unable to fulfill consumer demands.

Why is this? They may not be able to provide sufficiently low mileage. With each succeeding year, an increasing number of consumers seek a more efficient way to meet their energy needs. This manifests in the form of hybrid vehicles and those that do not rely on gas at all.

In these situations, if the business cannot satisfy consumer needs, how can they operate successfully?

They cannot, and that is the same fate that could befall virtually any business. Unless your business can remain green, growing, and exploring new avenues, it will not meet the needs of the consumer who, of course, is the lifeblood of the business.

How To Do It?

The inquiry that you need to reflect upon, then, is what actions must you take to realize this in your enterprise?

Assume that you operate an online business. Perhaps one of the crucial responsibilities you have is to stay abreast of search engine optimization.

If you do not adhere to and remain informed about the updated guidelines and the evolving landscape, your site will not achieve a good ranking and will lose its relevance.

In this context, it is critical that you sustain your knowledge and skills at the utmost level. This principle applies to various other enterprises, including insurance agencies and real estate firms. Unless you keep your expertise at a premium, you cannot ensure that you are acting correctly.

There are alternative considerations that you should contemplate as well. For instance, what about your marketing strategies? If your marketing approaches are not sufficiently contemporary (or if they are excessively modern for the wrong demographic), you may encounter difficulties.

In this situation, it is vital for you to discover a method to reach the appropriate audience with the suitable medium and to maintain that effort. You are already aware of how to promote your business; just ensure that you remain current on how to accomplish this as market dynamics evolve.

What other elements of your business can you identify that require your focus?

Discovering the various ways to stay innovative may involve keeping your product up to date, utilizing the latest technology and features to address consumer demands, and even reinventing yourself to guarantee that the business consistently remains at the forefront.

When you allocate time and resources towards staying relevant, the business continuously holds the opportunity for achievement.

Comprehending The Constantly Evolving Consumer

One of the most challenging tasks that you will face as an entrepreneur is ensuring that you satisfy your consumers' requirements. The challenging aspect of this is not the necessity to do it, but rather the method through which you grasp your consumer's preferences.

Certain companies invest millions in research annually to ensure that their product or sales proposition will resonate positively within the market. The alarming reality is that even with such investments, they still face significant risks and frequently encounter failures in their endeavors.

This can leave the small business owner questioning how they can possibly afford to achieve this.

Grasping the consumer's needs is not a straightforward endeavor. It is imperative that someone diligently seeks out this information, however.

If you wish, you can accomplish this by employing a company to conduct your marketing research. This could be a wise choice that is offered at a reasonable price to you. Based on your particular business and product, along with your marketing budget, this might be a suitable option for you.

On the flip side, it might not be something you want to pursue. In such a scenario, it's important to dedicate some time to discovering the right solution through alternative avenues. Regardless of whether you engage with your customers one-on-one or observe market trends related to your competitors, the aim is to ensure you consistently provide the best product available.

To confirm that you are competitive, evaluate your offerings against the other options available to consumers. What advantages do they possess that give them an edge over you?

Once you can address that and then confront it, you will be competitive and progressing, progressing towards profitability, naturally.

Chapter 4: Understanding Your Market

One point that needs to be addressed is that the market you are dealing with is likely to be quite different from the market that someone else encounters. The objectives you set in relation to the objectives of another person vary significantly. Indeed, you will likely find yourself pursuing advantages that are not aligned with your business goals.

To begin with, take a step back, remove yourself from the scenario, and examine your market.

If you are conducting sales online, observe the other sellers. If you are a small local business proprietor, take a moment to assess your local market.

Regardless of what you are engaged in, take a step back.

To Consider Now

The market you operate within is greatly influenced by who your customers are. If you are aiming for quick success, merely opening your business can get you started. However, by examining your market, you can gain insight into several aspects.

Ask yourself and respond to these questions before proceeding further.

• Who is my customer? Is it seniors or children, businesswomen or business owners…identify who your customer base is.

• How do they discover you? Do they locate you online, through a straightforward web search? Do they need to connect with you via an affiliate link? Do they find you in their local vicinity, in one of the busiest parts of the city?

• Who else exists in your market? Who stands as your competition? Where are they situated? What do they provide that gives you a competitive edge? In what ways do they outperform you in the marketplace? Why are they in business, taking customers away from you?

• What do you provide that is superior, in some aspect, to what your competitors offer? What do they present that surpasses what you offer in some way?

• Where is your market heading? Is the economy expanding, stagnating, or remaining stable? What financial resources do your customers possess for purchasing your product?

You could continue indefinitely with considerations regarding your particular business. Comprehending your market is vital to grasping what your future holds.

If you are unaware of who your consumer is, how can you anticipate their evolution?

Moreover, it is essential to understand what to expect from the surrounding market. If you observe the economy declining, it might be necessary to retreat and re-evaluate your future approach.

If, upon reviewing your market, you notice that your competition has adapted your product differently and is finding success, it is essential to take action. How will you compete? What will you provide that is improved? Furthermore, how will you advance towards success? How will you surpass them?

Paying Attention Counts

By focusing on your market, you will enhance your decision-making. When considering the long-term objectives that you have established to sustain your business, it is crucial that you prioritize your market as one of your main concerns.

If you neglect to dedicate time to remain in that marketplace, or even to branch out from it, you will be unable and unwilling to make things succeed. The business cannot flourish or remain viable without continuous vigilance on the surrounding market.

In upcoming chapters, we will delve deeper into growth and how to visualize your future in this context. However, it is vital to recognize that you must monitor your market for indications that it requires more of your product or that there is a lack of interest in it.

There is no question that some of these actions are vital, though some might also be challenging to implement. Nevertheless, if you do not invest the necessary time to evaluate and comprehend your current customer base, how will you ever succeed?

Once more, you have the option to hire someone to handle this task on your behalf. However, you can and ought to think about not just doing this yourself but also augmenting your efforts with your own research and expertise.

Having a physical presence in your marketplace (even online) ensures that individuals can reach out to you. It enables you to experience your market directly and thus make informed choices.

Chapter 5: Trend Versus Trend Setter

Is your business a trend creator? Or, do you follow current trends?

If you are uncertain, think about how this impacts your future.

As a trend creator, you consistently stay ahead of the competition. What you do is admired by others, and not just on one occasion. If you can achieve this repetitively, meaning you set the trend, you can even establish a situation where others look to you to define the next trend.

Conversely, if you are following the trend, the situation is less favorable. You will need to catch up to the other product or business that is thriving. In the process, you have wasted valuable selling time. Additionally, you will always need to monitor your competitor for what will happen next, instead of controlling what that will be. This can actually be a difficult position to find oneself in.

Take a moment right now to reflect on where you fit into this scenario.

Do you usually follow another's lead, hoping that there will be enough resources available for you as well? Or, do you actively search for something fresh and exciting and attempt to integrate that into your business?

Depending on your current position, this should clarify how it influences your long-term objectives and your capacity to achieve the success you desire.

Long Term Trend?

We all understand that trends come and go. You should also acknowledge that not all of them are suited for every business. However, trends are an important consideration when assessing your long-term success.

As previously mentioned, the advantages of leading the trend in your market are not solely based on basic sales. Indeed, if you can attain a temporary monopoly on a product for a few days, weeks, or more, you will experience impressive sales opportunities.

Nonetheless, those sales are fleeting. In the short term, that is all that is significant. However, in this discussion, we are focusing on long-term goals.

If you are the trend creator, then your long-term advantages of being in this industry include having more capability and flexibility to establish the next trend.

Some businesses in the marketplace lack the ability to effectively meet their customers' needs. Some will only achieve success occasionally concerning trends. However, the company that can create several trends can ensure greater capability in the future to do the same.

When a company has other companies looking to it for the next trend, guess who is poised for long-term success?

Consider Your Reputation

This is the single element that contributes to shaping your identity as a business as well. Not every business can claim that they possess a strong reputation with their clients over an extended period. Nevertheless, those that do can nearly rely on a monopoly within their industry.

Consider the local shops that often remain open well beyond their prime. What makes these establishments such appealing destinations? It's due to their strong reputation for delivering success and for excelling with their offerings. Even if their merchandise is no longer in vogue, it is still something that is desired and required for its excellence. That helps to support genuine success within the market.

Certainly, your reputation comes into consideration for numerous reasons or aspects beyond just this. The truth is that it also becomes relevant when you assess aspects like customer service, pricing, positive community relationships, and more. All these factors contribute to what your reputation is, just to mention a few!

When you are reflecting on your long-term aspiration of success and having ample funds in your possession, how does your reputation factor in?

We discussed how this occurs with trendsetting, but it can extend beyond that. In today's offline environment, it is challenging to secure a decent cup of coffee without pleading. Regardless of whether you are online or offline with your product, however, you can reap numerous rewards and advantages simply by delivering excellent service.

Cultivating a reputation is crucial for sustained development. Yet, don't forget that a reputation can swing both ways (positive and negative!) Therefore, ensure that you have a strong foundation of satisfied customers in your marketplace. It will yield benefits for you today as well as far into the future.

Chapter 6: Principal: History

One aspect that numerous business owners often overlook is their own history and the importance of learning from it. By reflecting on how your history influences your future opportunities, you can better understand why it is crucial to dedicate considerable attention to this matter.

Do you learn from history?

Many of us can remember instances when our parents admonished us. "Don't repeat that!" "Learn from your errors." All of these lessons hold significant importance in the realm of business as well.

In this principle, which is vital to the success of your business, it is necessary to consider your past and its journey to assist you in determining the direction of you and your business.

Questions To Consider

Now, to begin with this principle, reflect on these questions.

1. Where have you been and what insights have you gained? When pondering the past, clarify what it means to achieve success in this manner. What experiences do you possess that have imparted lessons relevant to your life and well-being today?

2. What lessons have you drawn from errors? Every entrepreneur encounters mistakes while navigating their business journey. Whether you are a newcomer or an experienced professional, errors can occur for various reasons. However, the key difference lies in whether you permit it to recur. If not, then finding success can be much more straightforward and quicker than if you continually repeat the same mistakes.

3. What do you wish you had done differently? Regrets need not be ignored. As an entrepreneur, you may have numerous regrets in mind. You might feel you have wasted a significant amount of time establishing your business. Now, take that regret and think about what you would change today. Would you initiate your business earlier? Invest more resources earlier?

Grasping these elements of your history can aid you in the long run. Certainly, we wish to avoid repeating the same mistakes, but few business owners manage to do this consistently.

Instead, most of us learn from our errors, but only if we take the time to analyze them and understand what they were and how they might be prevented.

Your history is uniquely yours. Whether considering your personal life history along with your business or the business alone, it is crucial to pause, reflect, and learn.

Making mistakes today can be challenging. No one desires to make them, but if it occurs, take the following steps.

1. Recognize that something went awry. Try not to feel frustration about it (if you can!) and acknowledge that something was amiss.

2. Identify what it was and ascertain how it occurred. Gaining the complete narrative, understanding the entire puzzle will enable better comprehension. Understanding how it transpired allows you to see intricately what the error was.

3. Choose to enhance your likelihood of preventing that mistake from occurring again. To achieve this, ensure that you allocate the required time making choices to avert this issue.

All Histories Are Not Bad

It is essential to acknowledge that history isn't always required to depict the negative aspects of circumstances. You can and should recognize the positive occurrences that have taken place in your history as well. What elements contributed to your current level of success? What factors led to that initial sale transpiring successfully?

Examining the positive events that have unfolded in the past is a fundamental principle of seeking answers for your future from the past. They help you recognize a genuine advantage in the positive outcomes within your business. You might even observe the methods through which the good occurred, allowing it to repeat itself continuously in your business's future as well.

By dedicating time to evaluate both the favorable and unfavorable events that transpired in your past, you can ensure that the advantages emerge in the future while the errors do not.

As a component of your future success, it is crucial to

comprehend your history and how to safeguard the future using this vast wealth of knowledge that you possess. Whether you realize it or not, this represents a personal insight and experience that no one else can replicate.

Chapter 7: Investing In Knowledge

If you resemble many entrepreneurs, then you understand that possessing a substantial amount of knowledge is critical for effectively managing your business.

As we have discussed, it is vital to ensure that the individuals offering you essential information are doing so without depleting your finances merely to enable you to invest more.

For instance, some of the most frequent errors made by entrepreneurs who are just beginning is that they continuously purchase information. This tendency is particularly evident among those launching an online business.

There is certainly no doubt that you need to acquire a significant amount of knowledge to bring your plans to fruition. You must understand how to initiate your endeavors, the steps needed to advance, and precisely where to execute everything. However, there is a boundary.

One aspect to consider is your capacity to make decisions. Once you have acquired the latest comprehensive kit, recognize that you are prepared to make certain choices.

If you buy one kit or program and then discover another that appears to offer extra advantages, you might feel inclined to buy that one as well. After all, having more information can't possibly be detrimental, can it?

It does not harm to possess a significant amount of information, except perhaps for your finances, of course. However, that is not the issue. The problem lies in how you utilize it.

A Principle

There are several actions you can take to achieve this. Keep this principle in mind.

If you catch yourself acquiring one product after another, you are not contemplating your next effective move, but rather impeding your progress.

If you obtain a product to enhance your business, it is crucial for you to utilize it and maximize its potential before proceeding to your next acquisition.

Making It Count

In subsequent chapters, we will discuss the importance of closely managing your finances, but for now, understand that the investment in any asset or tool intended to aid your business must be fully utilized for it to be considered a wise investment.

Regardless of the type of business you operate, if you do not allocate time to wisely invest in a business product, you are effectively squandering your profits.

If you succumb to all those schemes urging you to buy this incredible kit or that guaranteed method of earning a million dollars, you are indeed aiding someone else in achieving that million dollars.

Now, this is not to imply that you should refrain from purchasing any of them. Instead, choose the one that offers the most valuable resources for you, invest in it wisely, and then employ it thoroughly, integrating all necessary components into the plan. When you engage in this, your investment becomes advantageous for your business. If you simply proceed to the next task, you may encounter not advantages but obstacles and an empty wallet alongside it.

Making Wise Choices

In the upcoming chapters, we will discuss some crucial assets including your cash flow. However, before we get there, we must address the principle of making appropriate decisions about your business.

How do you approach decision-making? Do you make impulsive choices based on how you feel on any given day?

Do you exert excessive effort in seeking the ideal solution, so much so that by the time you reach a decision, it's already too late?

If you find yourself doing these things, you are not aiding your business but rather allowing circumstances to unfold as they will. This poses a significant challenge for the vast majority of newly starting entrepreneurs. Making sound decisions is challenging, but it must be accomplished, nonetheless.

Once you recognize how you are currently making decisions, you can start to amend it. To assist you in making the correct choices, adhere to these steps and tips for ensuring the right decisions do not slip by you.

Decision Making Tips

Making a choice requires effort. Here are some suggestions to assist you.

1. Devote time to understanding the potential product or issue you are encountering. If you are contemplating whether to buy a product, think about how it will improve your business's performance. What benefits can it offer you?

2. Allocate time to investigate possible solutions, encompassing both what you have discovered and what remains unknown. What can it resolve for your problem? What is the lowest price you can find? What are the potential drawbacks of this item?

3. After completing this research, evaluate if the investment is worthwhile for your well-being or that of your business. Waiting until you gather additional information about the product will enable a decision to emerge as a result of your research.

4. If you cannot reach a decision within a few days, then perhaps you are too hesitant about this item or choice to conclude it is suitable for your business. Let it go and move on. Alternatively, seek another option. Do not fixate on it.

Making appropriate decisions also entails recognizing your present circumstances.

If your business is not generating profits due to a lack of essential tools, it is essential to invest in new tools; otherwise, your business may not last long enough for you to be concerned about it.

If your business is performing adequately with no issues, then do not invest in something that does not provide a direct return on your profit margin.

Most entrepreneurs encounter numerous individuals coming to them, presenting a variety of different advantages, products, and services because, similar to you, they are aiming to make their business thrive. Don't be deceived by these attractions and shrewd businesspeople who believe they can resolve your issues.

While it might appear challenging to make sound choices regarding the business you own, it is essential that you develop confidence in yourself. If you lack trust in your decisions, you cannot manage a business.

This is also a principle that you must understand: If you do not have faith in yourself, you cannot ruin a prosperous business.

Chapter 8: Growth Success Without Potential Waste

One of the long-term considerations for every business owner is growth.

Growth refers to the advancement of your business to a higher level. This might involve broadening your business to offer additional products, diversify your services, or physically expand by establishing more locations.

Growth possesses the potential for the highest success over the long haul. An entrepreneur can achieve numerous advantages for themselves if they can navigate growth cautiously, avoiding going too far or spreading resources too thin too rapidly.

If this seems challenging, it can be. Many businesses have collapsed due to rapid expansion without securing enough market share to sustain them. Conversely, numerous businesses exist that have not capitalized on their growth potential and are now forgoing the possibility of higher profit margins.

It's Personal Too

Naturally, the growth of your business is a personal decision. Not everyone can ascertain where they stand in this regard at the start of their business journey. Nevertheless, one fact remains evident.

Your growth potential closely correlates with your sense of security in your business. If you possess trust and confidence that your business is worthwhile, then you can certainly pursue growth. However, if uncertainty prevails and you find it difficult to make decisions regarding your business's expansion, it simply cannot advance.

While many individuals are eager and prepared to seize any opportunity to enhance what they have built, others are content to let circumstances unfold without interference.

A crucial principle to bear in mind is that to achieve success in your business, you must assess your level of risk security. What risks are you comfortable with, and how can you ensure that your actions will yield long-term returns?

These questions may be difficult to tackle but are necessary to address.

Growing Too Fast

One of the most detrimental actions you can take for your business is to grow too quickly. If you lack the assets and cash flow to support such significant expansion, you may encounter various issues merely trying to maintain your business instead of focusing on its growth.

The danger of failing due to rapid overexpansion is that you might struggle to manage the responsibilities of multiple locations or a large corporation. Many large companies that have encountered this predicament have fallen apart because of the tremendous costs associated with acquiring additional buildings, payrolls, and units.

However, the smaller business owner does not confront the same extensive array of risks as larger corporations. But! It is essential to ensure that you invest thoughtfully in growth and not without first allocating time to it. Identifying where your potential gains lie is the first step toward success. Furthermore, a thorough assessment of the available possibilities is necessary.

Are You Prepared to Expand?

Individuals keen on discovering the optimal growth solutions are on the right track. However, keep in mind that making a decision requires being in the correct frame of mind and having conducted adequate research beforehand.

Regarding growth, the appropriate choice is ultimately up to you personally. Reflect on these inquiries concerning your success:

1. Does your business possess the cash flow to sustain not only your current location (or business) but also an additional one?

2. If you are undergoing expansion, what leads you to think that this growth will benefit your business?

3. What are the anticipated costs of growing, and does the business have the necessary resources to safeguard and cover those expenses?

All these factors are vital to your business's success concerning growth. Additionally, you must ensure that you do not constrain your growth due to insufficient opportunities as well.

Avoid Constraining Growth

Many business owners err by hesitating to step out and expand promptly or at all. While avoiding rapid movement is crucial, it is equally important to evaluate whether you are progressing too slowly to achieve benefits.

To grasp this aspect, you must again focus on your business. Are you extracting all that you can from it? Can you enhance your bottom line or achieve more if you pursue growth in some capacity?

To ascertain the appropriate level of growth for your business, consider conducting test market studies, investing in surveys, or simply starting gradually and building up. The investment you make in your business truly depends on you and how well the business has performed up to now.

A poorly performing business in one location may not succeed elsewhere either.

Conversely, a successful business that does not expand may face limitations.

Naturally, the reverse scenario can also apply. Research serves as the most effective method for gauging growth potential within your business.

Chapter 9: Managing Money Principles

What contributes to your profitability as a business owner? In the subsequent chapter, we will explore the various ways in which you need to oversee your cash flow and assets if you aim to have money in your pocket over the long run.

Do you possess the capability to contemplate, assess, and ultimately make business-related decisions?

As we have noted, your capacity to accomplish these tasks is what will either impede you or propel you forward today and in the future. Now, take those concepts and evaluate how well they correspond to your capability to make decisions about your business success where it truly matters: the profit margin.

Throughout this chapter, we will discuss several facets in detail, enabling you to gain a complete understanding of what you must do to achieve success concerning your business's profitability.

Controlling Your Money, Correctly

Do you have the necessary skills to oversee your finances? If you do not, it is time to seek someone who can and will handle it for you. Without strict oversight of the financials in your business, the future remains uncertain. This does not imply that you cannot part with money. This is a significant error that individuals tend to make.

Instead, as the entrepreneur and business owner, you need to learn to allocate your finances appropriately.

The first step for you is to establish a budget for your business's success. This should start with a comprehensive budget. Factors to consider include:

• Overseeing expenses that will keep the business operating smoothly.

• Managing your business's debt from growth or startup costs (to effectively pay them down.)

• Handling profit, if available, with a focus on how much will be reinvested back into the business and what will cater to other essential needs the business has.

The budget should be created meticulously, with considerable thought given to each of these areas. Rather than a dollar amount, the budget for the business should be expressed in percentages.

For instance, 20 percent of the profit may be allocated towards reinvestment in the business while the remainder will be directed toward reducing debt. Any percentages you feel comfortable with should be taken into account here.

In addition to the budgeting element of managing funds, the

organizational aspects must also be addressed. High-quality, thorough accounting and bookkeeping need to be maintained to manage the business's overall success and funds precisely.

Furthermore, measures must be implemented to handle unforeseen expenses and to ensure that everything is accurately accounted for.
Although it may seem clear to point out, numerous businesses fail due to inadequate financial management in their initial phases. Avoid falling for the "I don't have time now, I will do it later" deception. Without addressing this from the outset, it will not transpire throughout your business.

Don't Think You Need To?

If you believe that detailed accounting of your business is unnecessary, you are setting yourself up for significant failure. This is not to imply that you cannot achieve profitability while being disorganized, but keep in mind that we are discussing long-term success here.

Even massive, global corporations are extremely cautious about where every dollar they spend goes. After all, this is capital that could be utilized for the business, correct? It doesn't matter if your budget consists of hundreds of dollars or billions; effective money management is crucial for successfully sustaining any business during prosperous and challenging times.

Moreover, ensure that you are also keeping track of these figures. It does not benefit you to establish a system and use it if you do not maximize its effectiveness. The reality is that you should be doing the following:

• Identify where your money is going and ensure it is being tracked accurately.

- Identify areas where you can reduce costs and expenses.

- Identify what changes you can implement to spend less without compromising on the actual quality of your business.

Being somewhat frugal with your business is not negative, provided that you address all aspects of the business's needs, including reinvestment and potential for growth.

Your Cash Flow

The next principle of money management that you need to consider is your cash flow. Without a healthy cash flow in your business, it will fail.

If you are a small business owner, it is even more crucial to manage this, as there is no safety net or support behind you for a poor year or a significant setback that may occur. Loans only go so far, and they are ineffective if you cannot obtain them.

The capacity to sustain your cash flow is essential for having a successful and enduring business. Without your diligent management of cash flow, your business will struggle to survive during lean times or even during more prosperous periods.

How do you achieve this? There are several factors that you need to take into account here.

First and foremost, ensure that as an entrepreneur, you have a solid grip on the cash flow of your business. You should be able to personally oversee it every single day.

Does this seem excessive? If you fail to do this, you cannot truly understand where your business is positioned on any particular day. That could result in possible long-term issues with your success.

Carefully evaluate every expenditure you make. As a business owner, it is essential to make these choices judiciously. Just as expanding too quickly can be detrimental, so can lacking the cash flow necessary to sustain your business in the short or long term.

Additionally, you should oversee your budget, expenses, profits, and your capability to utilize every dollar you possess wisely. After all, this is the purpose of having those budgets established. Apply them, remain diligent with them, and maximize the potential of each dollar.

Two Principles To Remember

When considering business success, you should keep these two principles in mind regarding money management.

First, think about this: You should only spend money when there is a possibility of generating income from that expenditure.

It's quite clear, isn't it? You should refrain from investing in your business, particularly as a small business owner, unless it enables you to generate more revenue as a direct outcome.

Secondly, reflect on this: "If it is not revenue, it is an expense."

How does this apply to the current business you are operating? Does it facilitate your ability to meet your financial obligations successfully? Do you make purchases without carefully considering where those dollars go? If it does not generate revenue for you, it qualifies as an expense.

Effectively managing your cash flow will allow your business to accumulate funds rather than deplete them. Successfully achieving this increases the potential for your business to sustain long-term success. If you aim to be present in the future, manage your cash effectively, paying attention to nearly every dollar you have.

It's Not Being Cheap, It's Being Smart

Even though it may seem like we are advising you to be frugal or stingy with your business, you must ensure that the money you are spending is being utilized wisely, without any waste.

How can you be frugal (that's a more fitting term!) in a way that enables you to achieve genuine success?

• Identify how every dollar of your business's budget is spent.

• Is this dollar being allocated in the most effective manner? Does the expenditure contribute positively to your bottom line?

• Is there a more advantageous way to utilize that dollar? Can you acquire more value with another company, service, or opportunity?

• Is there a method to save your money more effectively, yielding a better return?

These are inquiries that any business owner should contemplate each and every day during their tenure in business. What improvements can be made to save more within their business for its benefit?

Why undertake this?

How many millionaires or even billionaires have you come across that still use their old, worn-out vehicles? Why do they choose to do that when they are capable of acquiring far more attractive and costly cars?

It is not because they are unwilling to spend money or that they enjoy being cheap. The advantage here actually stems from their preference for saving. Setting aside cash for your business is an excellent approach to achieving true success because you will have those resources available repeatedly when necessary.

The founder of Wal-Mart, Sam Walton, had a net worth of $25 billion at one time in his career. Would you believe that despite that level of wealth, he still drove his old pickup truck to work every day? Practicing frugality has its benefits, as this is clearly what contributed to his net worth of $25 billion.

When you practice frugality, your business will thrive, year after year. If you are a spender, you won't have the resources to enable that to occur year after year, will you?

All of these money-saving and cash management strategies may not appear to be very significant to you. If that is true, you are either already implementing them and experiencing success, or you are in fact squandering money and not attaining the success that you desire.

Nevertheless, managing your finances wisely is one of the essential elements to your success in a small business. Each entrepreneur must dedicate time to this, or they will find themselves lacking the advantages that they desperately need.

Ultimately, is it worthwhile to be somewhat frugal to achieve that massive, multi-billion dollar net worth? There is no vehicle in this world that can offer you that kind of assurance, can it?

Ensure you incorporate these money management strategies and principles into your daily routine and long-term objectives within your business.

Chapter 10: Marketing For True Success

If you are an entrepreneur, marketing is inherently part of you; at least it ought to be there if you wish to attract customers at all.

However, do you promote your business for genuine success and lasting rewards?

If you believe you do, you might not fully grasp the real power of effective marketing tools.

What constitutes marketing? Marketing is what attracts a customer to your business. You need to ensure others know you are present and prepared to provide a service to them.

That fundamental definition alone is insufficient to guide you through the entire marketing process for your business success, however.

If you desire long-term success, treat marketing with greater seriousness and adhere to these suggestions for various marketing aspects.

Assess Your Product's Potential

Before achieving success in marketing your business, you need to dedicate considerable time to identifying what it is about your offering that others desire.

In other words, what benefit does your product provide? A thriving business will supply some form of immediate gratification for a need someone possesses. You should contemplate this even prior to starting a business. What issues can your product potentially resolve or what need can it satisfy?

Moreover, you must identify how it can provide these benefits to your customer in a way that enhances their life. Perhaps you can present them with a solution to a dilemma they face, but it is still a feasible option to address that solution.

Having a precisely defined benefit to market is crucial for maximally leveraging your product. People want to know, "What will it do for me?" and "Why should I choose this over an alternative?"

Once you ascertain how this influences your product's capabilities, you can determine the appropriate marketing strategy for that product. Addressing those inquiries is essential to achieving defined success in this area.

Pricing Is Important Too

The next factor to consider is that of pricing. In marketing, you might overlook the importance of the price you assign to your product, but it matters as well. People are motivated by discounts and deals. They appreciate a product that fulfills their need while being economical.

Without appropriate pricing, it doesn't matter how effectively you market the product in the end.

What do consumers seek regarding a product or service's pricing? They desire something reasonable, not something that will financially strain them. Additionally, most individuals recognize the necessity for a business to generate profit. The issue arises when they feel exploited.

In addition, competition is important here as well. If your product is superior to another, it may deserve a higher price, but it shouldn't be exorbitant because if it is, no one will pay attention to it.

Consider its capability of being identified as a Unique Selling Proposition. This implies that it will possess similar but at least some distinctive features that will enable it to be competitively priced against other products.

As we mentioned, your product must meet the needs of someone out there. However, if there are five different products fulfilling that need, it may be challenging for you to identify your niche. Therefore, you must develop a unique quality that will enhance your marketing and your pricing.

What distinguishes your product as better, in other words?

If you are a new business owner, for instance, and seeking a new product to invest in, you might not want to attempt to create your own product, service, or another element. Instead, you may simply conclude that taking an existing product from the market and discovering a way to improve it or offer a better price is the right approach.

Marketing Effectively

Throughout this chapter, we have discussed methods for successfully marketing your business. Now, consider your sales advantages.

Can you assert that when every one of your employees (or just yourself) enters the premises, their objective is to satisfy a customer?

Not merely to serve a customer but to also ensure their satisfaction. If you cannot assert that, then perhaps your marketing in sales terms may not be functioning as effectively as it ought to be.

Here's what we mean. If your intention is to generate a profit, then your goal is to maximize the business you receive.

However, what if you aimed to delight every customer? In that case, you would not only secure that sale, but you would also ensure that customer keeps returning repeatedly.

Since we are considering long-term objectives and success, it is logical to ensure that your sales goal is to excel at what you do in order to satisfy your customer to such an extent that they do not even think of going elsewhere for their needs.

In your business, you need to focus your marketing and sales strategies on both creating and retaining your customer.

Sales For Success

To advance this further, you must also reflect on your selling skills. As an accomplished entrepreneur, it is essential to thoughtfully assess how you are selling, how well it functions, and how you can enhance it both in the short run and the long run.

If you are unable to sell, you will not achieve success in your business. Simply put, your journey ends here.

Initially, as the owner of the business, you need to be capable of promoting yourself. Do you embody the qualities of a business person who is:

- Approachable
- Likeable
- Friendly
- Educated
- Dedicated?

Or are you the individual they all avoid when they step through your door? Presenting yourself as a reliable source of information and products is the most effective way to establish yourself as the go-to individual.

Moreover, you are also required to sell your product convincingly to your customer. This aspect is also interconnected with marketing your business for success.

In summary, if you cannot effectively sell your business, then you have no place in the business world. Learn to feel enthusiasm for your own product. Then, acquire the skills to sell it successfully to those around you.

You must accomplish this task prior to motivating or training someone else to do it on your behalf. Being enthusiastic, energized, positive, and truly invigorating is the ideal approach in this scenario. If you are not comfortable discussing your product or business with your closest friends, how can you possibly sell it to a total stranger?

Here's the essence of marketing and sales. If you cannot excel at promoting your product and getting others to perceive it as you do, then success will remain out of reach.

Sales proficiency is crucial for sales to occur. Achieving sales equates to having customers who will return to you. This translates to long-term success for you as a business owner.

Chapter 11: Principles To Remember And Use

1. Launch your business with a focus on your long-term prosperity.

2. Establish and uphold objectives that align with long-term aims.

3. Handle growth prudently, ensuring it supports your long-term advantages.

4. Comprehend your market and your place within it.

5. Be the trendsetter, but do so with caution.

6. Take lessons from both the positive and negative experiences of your past.

7. Invest wisely, and make informed decisions as well.

8. Expand judiciously without incurring excess.

9. Oversee your finances wisely, stringently, frugally, and with care.

10. Learn to promote your business accurately and efficiently.

Conclusion

In a society that prioritizes immediate concerns, it is vital for your own welfare to look ahead to your future.

By implementing prudent business practices such as those discussed in this e-book, your objectives tend to be quite advantageous. Not only can you achieve success for your business now, but the future sustainability of your business becomes more assured.

A business represents an investment and can certainly go in either direction (profitable or unprofitable.) When you commence with a strong foundation, offering the right resources, knowledge, and a few guiding principles for managing your business, you increase your chances of advancing positively in your business endeavors.

It does not matter whether your business is extensive and worth billions or a fledgling enterprise just starting out. The aim is to provide it with the nurturing principles that contribute to its growth and success.

If you take the time to evaluate, operate, and then reassess each of these facets in your business, the ultimate outcome will be success.

It is your money. You have the freedom to spend it however you choose. Applying these essential principles will assist you in cultivating a successful business that generates income for you over the years by maintaining a presence in the market.

www.ingramcontent.com/pod-product-compliance
Lightning Source LLC
Chambersburg PA
CBHW030055230526
45471CB00003B/1105